PASSWORD 3

Teacher's Manual with Tests

Lynn Bonesteel

Boston University

Longman

Password 3: A Reading and Vocabulary Text

Pearson Education, 10 Bank Street, White Plains, NY 10606

Teacher's Manual with Tests by Lynn Bonesteel

Executive editor: Laura Le Dréan
Development editor: Andrea Bryant
Senior production editor: Jane Townsend
Marketing manager: Joe Chapple
Senior manufacturing buyer: Dave Dickey
Cover design: Tracey Cataldo
Text design: Ann France, Patricia Wosczyk
Digital layout specialist: Lisa Ghiozzi
Text font: 11.5/13 Minion

ISBN: 0-13-140894-1

Printed in the United States of America   5 6 7 8 9 10 -OPM- 08

LONGMAN ON THE **WEB**

Longman.com offers online resources for teachers
and students. Access our Companion Websites, our
online catalog, and our local offices around the world.

Visit us at **longman.com.**

CONTENTS

INTRODUCTION

This manual contains:

- the **Answer Key** for all exercises in the student book.

- six **Unit Tests and answers**. Each unit test includes a short reading (approximately 350 words) on the theme of the unit and sections that test comprehension, reading skills practiced in the unit, and vocabulary from all three chapters.

- the **Quick Oral Review**. The Quick Oral Review offers sets of prompts you can use for rapid vocabulary drills. These drills can be an important part of the spaced repetition of vocabulary— repeated exposures to newly learned words at increasing intervals—that helps students remember the words they learn. A few minutes of rapid-fire review can be a lively way to get a class started, and it can also be a useful way to wind up a lesson or review vocabulary for a unit test. To do one of these drills, have students look back at the list of target vocabulary from a chapter you have completed. Prompts are given here for ten of the words or phrases. Call out a prompt to the class; students then find or say the word as quickly as possible. The prompts given in this manual are brief definitions, which you can add to as needed. You can also give students unfinished sentences (e.g., "The school wanted to ask a lot of students about their new classes, so they sent out a . . ." to elicit *survey*) or examples (e.g., "Computers, cell phones, and fax machines are examples of . . ." to elicit *technology*). More demanding tasks for a review drill would include giving the target word or phrase and asking students to give an example of it, use it in a sentence, or explain its meaning. Quick Oral Reviews should be just that—quick—and should be repeated as needed in later classes.

References

Butler, M. (2001, October). First Gene Linked to Speech Identified. *Science, 294,* 32. [Electronic version]

Haitch, R. (1985, December 1). Child Inventor. *The New York Times,* p. 58. [Electronic version]

Kurzweil Technologies, Inc. (n.d.). A Biography of Ray Kurzweil. Retrieved June 24, 2004 from http://www.kurzweiltech.com/raybio.html

Masson, J. (1995). *When Elephants Weep: The Emotional Lives of Animals.* New York City, NY: Dell Publishing.

MOBA: Art Too Bad To Be Ignored. (n.d.). Retrieved June 24, 2004 from http://www.museumofbadart.org/about/index.html

Office of the Surgeon General. (n.d.). Overweight in Children and Adolescents. Retrieved June 24, 2004 from http://www.surgeongeneral.gov/topics/obesity/calltoaction/fact_adolescents.html

Platt, W. (1996, March 17). Kids Show Ingenuity Is Mother of Invention. *St. Petersburg Times,* p. 1. [Electronic version]

Rourke, B. (2003, December 2). The Bathroom Beckons—Good Taste, Talent Not Allowed at Museum of Bad Art. *Providence Journal-Bulletin,* p. G1. [Electronic version]

The Seeing Eye. (n.d.). History of Seeing Eye Dogs. Retrieved June 24, 2004 from http://www.seeingeye.org/GuidedTour.asp?sc=hs#2t

Tangley, L. (2000, October 30). Animal Emotions. *U.S. News and World Report.* [Electronic version]

STUDENT BOOK ANSWER KEY

Answers not given will vary.

UNIT 1: Artistic Innovations

CHAPTER 1: What Is Anime?

GETTING READY TO READ, PAGE 2

Ⓑ

1. b   4. b
2. a   5. b
3. a

READING

Comprehension Check, Page 5

Corrections for false items may vary. The number in parentheses is the paragraph number where the correct information can be found.

2. F—Manga are comic books; anime is animation. Anime developed from manga. The characters in anime first appeared in manga.(1–2)
3. T
4. T
5. F—Important characters sometimes die in anime. (3)
6. T

EXPLORING VOCABULARY

Thinking about the Vocabulary, Page 5

Guessing Strategy

Answers may vary but should contain content similar to the following: **Popularity** means *the quality of being liked or supported by a large group of people.*

Using the Vocabulary, Page 6

1. related   6. moral
2. got their start   7. challenges, rapid
3. popularity   8. beauty
4. reportedly   9. original
5. involved

DEVELOPING READING SKILLS

Understanding Topics and Main Ideas, Page 7
1. Anime
2. a

UNDERSTANDING CAUSE AND EFFECT, PAGE 8
Answers will vary. Possible answers include:

2. the artwork is beautiful, and anime deals with complex subjects and characters.
3. the characters and situations are morally complex, and death is shown as a natural part of life.
4. what you hear does not match the mouth movements, and hearing the spoken (and sung) Japanese is part of the cultural experience and beauty of anime.
5. they fall in love with Japan and the beautiful Japanese language.

EXPANDING VOCABULARY

Using the Vocabulary in New Contexts, Page 8
1. reportedly   6. original
2. challenges   7. related
3. moral   8. involved
4. got his start   9. rapid
5. popularity   10. beauty

Word Families, Page 9
1. technological
2. popularity
3. rapidly
4. morally
5. originality

CHAPTER 2: The Scientist and the Stradivarius

GETTING READY TO READ, PAGE 12

Ⓑ

1. e   4. c
2. a   5. b
3. d

READING

Comprehension Check, Page 15

Corrections for false items may vary. The number in parentheses is the paragraph number where the correct information can be found.

2. ?
3. T
4. F—The chemicals in the wood and varnish of Stradivari instruments are very important to the way they sound. (6)
5. F—Stradivari probably did not know why his violins had such a remarkable sound. (6)
6. ?

EXPLORING VOCABULARY

Thinking about the Vocabulary, Page 16

Guessing Strategy

artistic: P   brilliant: P   illiterate: N

Using the Vocabulary, Page 17

1. laboratory
2. illiterate
3. remarkable
4. brilliant
5. artistic, due to
6. announcement
7. theory
8. beliefs
9. stands by
10. proof

DEVELOPING READING SKILLS

Understanding Topics and Main Ideas, Page 18

Answers will vary. Possible answers include:
1. why Stradivari instruments have such a remarkable sound
2. Using science, Joseph Nagyvary believes that he has discovered the reason that Stradivari instruments have such a remarkable sound.

Scanning, Page 18

1. violas, cellos, and guitars
2. No, he wasn't. Two of his sons and other violin makers from Cremona did too.
3. in 1977
4. two violins: a Stradivarius and a Nagyvarius (a violin made by Dr. Nagyvary)

Understanding Inference, Page 19

1. a
2. a
3. a

EXPANDING VOCABULARY

Using the Vocabulary in New Contexts, Page 19

1. illiterate
2. Due to
3. proof
4. announcement
5. laboratory
6. belief
7. stand by
8. artistic
9. theory
10. remarkable
11. brilliant

Word Families, Page 20

Ⓐ
1. -er, -ist
2. -ment, -ry
3. -ic, -al
4. announce

Ⓑ
1. announce
2. announcer
3. artist
4. chemical
5. chemistry
6. artistry

Studying Word Grammar, Page 21

Ⓐ
1. because
2. due to
3. so
4. Due to

CHAPTER 3: The History of Rap

GETTING READY TO READ, PAGE 23

Ⓑ
1. performer
2. spinning
3. scratched
4. equipment

READING

Comprehension Check, Page 26

Corrections for false items may vary. The number in parentheses is the paragraph number where the correct information can be found.

2. T
3. F—Rap got its start in the Bronx in New York City. (2)
4. T
5. F—Many rappers perform with live musicians. (1)
6. T

EXPLORING VOCABULARY

Thinking about the Vocabulary, Page 27

Guessing Strategy
1. **Live** means *not recorded.*
2. **Characteristic** means *special quality.*

Using the Vocabulary, Page 28

1. a
2. b
3. b
4. b
5. c
6. b
7. a
8. c
9. b
10. b
11. c
12. c
13. b

DEVELOPING READING SKILLS

Scanning, Page 30

Ⓐ
b. 1
c. 5
d. 6
e. 4
f. 2
g. 7

Ⓑ *Page 30*

Answers will vary. Possible answers include:

Paragraph 2: No one is sure, but most people think that rap got its start in the Bronx in New York City in the 1960s.

Paragraph 3: The DJs and the MCs are the performers in rap. They speak louder than the music and interact with the crowd when they perform.

Paragraph 4: Grandmaster Flash is a DJ who invented techniques that have become an important part of rap music and hip-hop culture.

Paragraph 5: In the 1970s and 1980s, rap became more and more popular. The DJs competed with each other, and their rhymes became more clever.

Paragraph 6: People all over the world listen to rap. One of the reasons for its popularity is that it gives young people the chance to express themselves.

Paragraph 7: You don't need a lot of equipment or training to be a rapper, but it is not easy. It calls for many skills.

Understanding Topics and Main Ideas, Page 30

Answers may vary but should contain content similar to the following:

Rap music is a very interesting form of music with a fascinating history.

EXPANDING VOCABULARY

Using the Vocabulary in New Contexts, Page 31

1. personality
2. calls for
3. interact
4. stands out
5. technique
6. clever
7. rhyme
8. competing
9. contributes
10. expression
11. characteristics
12. live
13. grew out of

Word Families, Page 32

expression, performance, interaction, competition, contribution, fascination

B

1. performance
2. competition
3. interaction
4. contribution
5. expression
6. fascination

Studying Phrasal Verbs, Page 33

1. really stand out
2. stand by
3. calls for

UNIT 1 Wrap-Up

REVIEWING READING SKILLS AND VOCABULARY

Comprehension Check, Page 35

Corrections for false items may vary. The number in parentheses is the paragraph number where the correct information can be found.

1. T
2. ?
3. F (3–4)
4. T
5. F (5)

Guessing Meaning from Context, Page 36

Answers may vary but should contain content similar to the following:

a school, especially one that trains students in a special art or skill

Understanding Inference, Page 36

1, 3, 5

Scanning, Page 36

Answers will vary. Possible answers include:

1. he was a brilliant and very original artist.
2. during that time he painted only with the color blue.
3. it is considered to be the first cubist painting.
4. the beauty, complexity, and originality of his artwork live on in the many works he left behind.

EXPANDING VOCABULARY

Studying Phrasal Verbs, Page 37

1. c
2. d
3. a
4. b

Word Families, Page 38

Noun (person): -er, -ist

Noun (not a person): -ance, -ion, -ity, -ment, -tion, -try

Adjective: -al, -ic

B

1. involvement
2. relevance
3. complexity
4. technical
5. theorist

PLAYING WITH WORDS, PAGE 39

Across
2. interact
6. expression
10. evil
11. proof
12. related
13. challenge
14. beauty

Down
1. laboratory
3. original
4. belief
5. announcement
7. scratch
8. reportedly
9. rapid

BUILDING DICTIONARY SKILLS

Finding Phrasal Verbs, Page 40

1. out
2. up
3. off
4. on

UNIT 2: The Challenges of Youth

CHAPTER 4: Sleepy Teens

GETTING READY TO READ, PAGE 43

(B)
1. experiment
2. patterns
3. depressed
4. in tears

READING

Comprehension Check, Page 47

Corrections for false items may vary. The number in parentheses is the paragraph number where the correct information can be found.
1. F—Often, teenagers don't get enough sleep. (4)
2. T
3. F—The brains of teenagers are different from the brains of adults. (4)
4. F—Teenagers cannot do their best schoolwork early in the morning. (6)
5. T
6. T

EXPLORING VOCABULARY

Thinking about the Vocabulary, Page 47

Guessing Strategy

The word *lowered* should be circled.

Using the Vocabulary, Page 48
1. official
2. stay up
3. complaint
4. concern
5. experts, lack
6. likely
7. at least
8. absences, reduced
9. dropout

DEVELOPING READING SKILLS

Understanding Main Ideas, Major Points, and Supporting Details, Page 49
1. a
2. 2. MP   4. SD   6. SD   8. SD mp
   3. SD   5. MP   7. SD

EXPANDING VOCABULARY

Using the Vocabulary in New Contexts, Page 50
1. expert
2. at least
3. stay up
4. likely
5. complaint
6. concern
7. reduce
8. lack
9. absences
10. dropout
11. official

Word Families, Page 51

Noun: absence, complaint, concern, experiment, official
Verb: reduced
Adjective: depressed, dropout

Noun: reduction, depression, officials
Verb: drop out, concerns, experimenting, complain
Adjective: absent, official

Studying Word Grammar, Page 52

(A)
1. fascinating
2. fascinated
3. challenging
4. challenged
5. threatened
6. threatening

CHAPTER 5: Growing Up Gifted

GETTING READY TO READ, PAGE ~~54~~ 55

(A) B
1. a
2. c
3. a
4. c

READING

Comprehension Check, Page 57

Corrections for false items may vary. The number in parentheses is the paragraph number where the correct information can be found.

1. F—Pascal Charbonneau does not enjoy the attention he gets for being a child prodigy. (1)
2. F—Most child prodigies know a lot about a variety of subjects. (1)
3. T
4. T
5. ?
6. F—Most musical prodigies do not become famous musicians (5)

EXPLORING VOCABULARY

Thinking about the Vocabulary, Page 58

Guessing Strategy

burn out: N   championship: P   critical: N

Using the Vocabulary, Page 59

1. Gifted
2. concentrate on
3. championships, literature
4. sensitive
5. injustice
6. critical
7. perfectionists
8. pressure
9. burn out
10. published
11. Despite

DEVELOPING READING SKILLS

Understanding Major Points, Page 60

Answers will vary. Possible answers include:

1. Everyone expects you to perform well all of the time. This is a lot of pressure for a young person to deal with. You never feel satisfied because you are trying to be perfect.
2. They can't deal with the pressure. Also, they are perfectionists, so they want to be at the top, but very few performers can make it to the top. If they can't be the star, they quit.
3. They are more intelligent and sensitive than their peers, so perhaps they are able to see things more clearly, including injustice. Also, perhaps because their "gifts" set them apart from others, they can relate to others who are treated unfairly because they are different in some way.

Understanding Supporting Details, Page 60

1. two to three years more advanced
2. between two and five percent

Understanding Inference, Page 60

1. Child prodigies are often unhappy because they always want to be perfect.
2. According to Francoys Gagne, many young musical prodigies are not happy having just an ordinary career as a musician.
3. Many gifted young musicians do not have successful careers, despite having remarkable talent.

EXPANDING VOCABULARY

Using the Vocabulary in New Contexts, Page 61

1. championship
2. burn out
3. published
4. sensitive
5. injustice
6. Despite
7. literature
8. perfectionist
9. concentrate on
10. pressure
11. gifted
12. critical

Word Families, Page 62

1. achievement
2. tendency
3. publisher
4. publication
5. criticize
6. criticism
7. critique
8. critique
9. concentration
10. pressure (or criticize)
11. champion
12. perfect
13. critic
14. perfection
15. perfect

Studying Word Grammar, Page 64

Ⓐ
1. publishing
2. burning out
3. criticizing
4. pressuring
5. achieving

CHAPTER 6: School Bullies

GETTING READY TO READ, PAGE 66

Ⓑ
1. b   2. c   3. d   4. a

READING

Comprehension Check, Page 69

Corrections for false items may vary. The number in parentheses is the paragraph number where the correct information can be found.

1. T
2. F—Bullies have many friends. (3)

3. F—Bullies have a lot of self-esteem. (3)
4. T
5. T
6. F—It is the responsibility of both parents and schools. (8–9)

EXPLORING VOCABULARY

Thinking about the Vocabulary, Page 69

Guessing Strategy

Answers may vary but should contain content similar to the following:

Examine means *to look at something carefully in order to make a decision, find out something, etc.*

Using the Vocabulary, Page 70

1. conducted
2. examines
3. data
4. survey
5. economic
6. background
7. overweight
8. anxious
9. self-esteem
10. attitude
11. freedom
12. contact
13. on the basis of

DEVELOPING READING SKILLS

Understanding Main Ideas, Page 72

Answers may vary but should contain content similar to the following:

Bullying is a serious problem in many schools. A Norwegian researcher named Dr. Olweus has developed a very effective program for dealing with the problem of school bullies.

Understanding Inference, Page 72

2. T   4. M   6. M   8. M
3. M   5. T   7. M

EXPANDING VOCABULARY

Using the Vocabulary in New Contexts, Page 72

1. attitude
2. examine
3. freedom
4. overweight
5. on the basis of
6. economic
7. anxious
8. data
9. survey
10. background
11. contact
12. self-esteem
13. conduct

Word Families, Page 74

Ⓐ

Noun (thing): anxiety, economy, examination/exam

Verb: survey, free, *economize*
Adjective: aggressive, free

UNIT 2 Wrap-Up

REVIEWING READING SKILLS AND VOCABULARY

Comprehension Check, Page 78

Corrections for false items may vary. The number in parentheses is the paragraph number where the correct information can be found.

1. T
2. F—The brain of a three-year-old is smaller than the brain of a teenager. (2)
3. ?
4. F—If a teenager doesn't use a particular part of the brain enough, the brain cells in that area will die off. (3)
5. T

Guessing Meaning from Context, Page 78

Answers may vary but should contain content similar to the following:

completely filled with

Understanding Main Ideas, Page 78

Answers may vary but should contain content similar to the following:

Scientists have discovered that the brains of teenagers are different from the brains of adults, and that behavior during the teen years affects the development of the brain.

Understanding Inference, Page 78

1. Until recently, scientists did not know exactly why teenagers behave the way that they do.
2. Experts do not believe anymore that the behavior of parents or changes in body chemistry are the causes of negative teenage behavior.
3. Experts think that parents should help their teenagers to develop healthy patterns of behavior.

EXPANDING VOCABULARY

Studying Word Grammar, Page 79

Answers may vary but should contain similar content.

2. do not put enough pressure on themselves to perform well. They don't achieve as much as they could.
3. the act of expressing your thoughts or feelings.

Studying Phrasal Verbs, Page 80

(A)
1. NO
2. O
3. NO

Word Families, Page 80

1. victimize
2. economize
3. publicize
4. criticize
5. pressurize

Playing with Words, Page 81

1. background
2. data
3. likely
4. aggression
5. absences
6. perfectionist
7. lack
8. survive
9. pattern
10. official
11. despite
12. gifted

BUILDING DICTIONARY SKILLS

Finding the Correct Meaning, Page 82

1. a. 1   b. 2
2. a. 2   b. 1   c. 3
3. a. 1   b. 2

UNIT 3: Genetics: The Science of Who We Are

CHAPTER 7: The Science of Genetics

GETTING READY TO READ, PAGE 85

(B)
1. b
2. a
3. b
4. c
5. a

READING

Comprehension Check, Page 88

Corrections for false items may vary. The number in parentheses is the paragraph number where the correct information can be found.

1. F—People did not know that children got their traits from both their mother and father. (1)
2. T
3. T
4. F—Our genes do have an effect on our behavior. (6)
5. F—Genetic engineering is used on all living things, including animals, humans, and plants. (7)
6. T

EXPLORING VOCABULARY

Thinking about the Vocabulary, Page 89

Guessing Strategy

treatment using the part of a cell that carries inherited traits

Using the Vocabulary, Page 90

1. realize, generation
2. genes, instructions
3. individual
4. come out
5. illnesses, cure
6. cell, replace
7. gender
8. determine
9. desirable

DEVELOPING READING SKILLS

Scanning, Page 91

a. 2
b. 5
c. 9
d. 1
e. 7
f. 6
g. 3
h. 4
i. 8

Summarizing, Page 91

Answers will vary. Possible answers include:

Paragraph 2: In the nineteenth century, an Austrian scientist named Gregor Mendel discovered how traits are passed from one generation to the next. The modern field of genetics grew out of the experiments he did on pea plants.

Paragraph 3: Mendel discovered that if you cross a short pea plant and a tall one, it will take two generations for another short pea plant to appear. From this discovery, he developed a theory involving dominant and recessive traits.

Paragraph 4: Future scientists applied what Mendel had discovered about the genes of pea plants to all living things, including humans.

Paragraph 5: We inherit our genes from our parents. They are like a set of instructions for how to make a human being.

Paragraph 6: Today, scientists are learning more about genes. They are using this knowledge in genetic engineering and genetic testing.

Paragraph 7: Through genetic engineering, scientists can remove genes that aren't working correctly from plants or animals, and replace them.

Paragraph 8: In human beings, doctors can use genetic testing to find out if someone has a genetic illness or is likely to get one. With some diseases, they can then use genetic engineering to replace the genes that are causing the problem.

Paragraph 9: In the future, scientists might be able to use genetic engineering to help parents choose the specific traits that they want their children to inherit.

EXPANDING VOCABULARY

Using the Vocabulary in New Contexts, Page 92

1. replace
2. instructions
3. cured
4. desirable
5. generations
6. genes
7. illness
8. realize
9. individual
10. cells
11. determines
12. came out
13. genders

Word Families, Page 93

Noun: desire, prevention, cure
Verb: desire
Adjective: preventable. curable

1. preventable
2. curable
3. desire
4. cure
5. prevention
6. desire

PUTTING IT ALL TOGETHER

Discussion, Page 94

1. The first and third news stories are true. The other two (at least at the time of publication) are not true.

CHAPTER 8: Designing the Future

GETTING READY TO READ, PAGE 96

Ⓑ
1. b
2. a
3. e
4. d
5. c

READING

Comprehension Check, Page 99

Corrections for false items may vary. The number in parentheses is the paragraph number where the correct information can be found.

1. ?
2. T
3. F—In the future, parents might be able to use genetic engineering to determine what their future child will look like. (2)
4. T
5. F—Probably many parents will use the technology. (4)
6. ?

EXPLORING VOCABULARY

Thinking about the Vocabulary, Page 99

Guessing Strategy

Answers may vary but should contain content similar to the following:

Shortage means *a situation in which there is not enough of something that people need.*

Using the Vocabulary, Page 100

1. approaching
2. athletic
3. intellect
4. brings up
5. shortage
6. acceptable
7. appearance
8. restricted
9. convinced
10. lead to, advantages
11. In short, humanity

DEVELOPING READING SKILLS

Understanding Inference, Page 102

1. The technology for designing babies does not exist yet.
2. Right now, scientists don't know how to make humans with animal traits.
3. Some geneticists think that it will be a long time before the technology that will allow parents to design their babies is developed.

Summarizing, Page 102

Summaries will vary but should contain similar content.

Because of genetic *engineering*, many scientists believe that in the future, parents will be able to *design their children. Already, scientists know how to use genetic engineering and genetic testing to treat some genetic illnesses, and to determine the gender of the fetus. In the future, scientists expect to be able to identify the genes that determine most human traits, including those that affect physical*

appearance, intellect, and personality. When that happens, surveys show that many parents *will use genetic engineering to choose desirable traits for their children.* The use of genetic engineering to "design" children leads to some difficult moral questions, for example: *Will the children of rich parents have more "design" advantages than the children of poor parents who can't afford genetic engineering?* But the most important question is: *Will genetic engineering change what it means to be human?*

EXPANDING VOCABULARY

Using the Vocabulary in New Contexts, Page 103

1. athletic
2. convinced
3. humanity
4. appearance
5. restricted
6. lead to
7. acceptable
8. bring up
9. intellect
10. advantages
11. In short
12. shortage
13. approach

Word Families, Page 104

1. a. 2, the first syllable
   b. 3, the second syllable
2. a. 3, the second syllable
   b. 4, the third syllable
3. a. 4, the second syllable
   b. 2, the first syllable

Studying Word Grammar, Page 105

1. Historically
2. humanely
3. In short
4. Actually

CHAPTER 9: A Drug to Match Your Genes

GETTING READY TO READ, PAGE 107

(B)

1. b
2. a
3. a
4. a
5. a
6. a

READING

Comprehension Check, Page 110

Corrections for false items may vary. The number in parentheses is the paragraph number where the correct information can be found.

1. T
2. T
3. T
4. T
5. F—Doctors can't now give a patient a drug that is designed just for him or her, not for any other person. (7)
6. T

EXPLORING VOCABULARY

Thinking about the Vocabulary, Page 110

Guessing Strategy

Answers may vary but should contain content similar to the following:

Beneficial means *good for you.*

Using the Vocabulary, Page 111

1. factor
2. diet
3. suffer, severe
4. harmful
5. effective, poison
6. in charge of
7. progressing

DEVELOPING READING SKILLS

Understanding Supporting Details, Page 112

1. Yes (paragraph 3)
2. No (paragraph 5)
3. No (paragraph 5)
4. It doesn't say.
5. No (paragraph 6)
6. Yes (paragraph 5)

Understanding Major Points, Page 112

Answers may vary but should contain similar content.

1. Because their genes are different, and they might be of different ages or have very different diets. One person's disease might be more severe than the other's, and they might be taking other drugs too.
2. Their genes are different.
3. Genes are in charge of how much of the drug your body will use, and how quickly it will use the drug. If your genes do not let your body use enough of the drug, it might not be effective for you. If your genes use the drug very slowly, it might stay in your body too long and poison you.
4. They might be designed specifically for each person's individual body chemistry.

EXPANDING VOCABULARY

Using the Vocabulary in New Contexts, Page 113

1. diet
2. harmful
3. progressed
4. poison
5. severe
6. effective
7. in charge of
8. suffering
9. factor

Word Families, Page 114

(A)

1. recovering
2. prescribe
3. intended
4. harmful
5. progressing

(B)

1. c
2. f
3. d
4. b
5. a

Studying Collocations, Page 115

(A)

1. suffers from
2. recovered from his illness
3. perform the operation
4. follow a strict diet

UNIT 3 Wrap-Up

REVIEWING READING SKILLS AND VOCABULARY

Comprehension Check, Page 117

Corrections for false items may vary. The number in parentheses is the paragraph number where the correct information can be found.

1. F—They had a way to develop healthier, faster-growing plants. (1)
2. T
3. F—They can't decide for themselves. (2)
4. T
5. ?

Guessing Meaning from Context, Page 118

Answers may vary but should contain similar content.

1. corn, rice, tomatoes, etc.
2. changed
3. the product name, the ingredients, the number of calories, etc.

Understanding Major Points, Page 118

Answers may vary but should contain similar content.

1. It is food that is grown from seeds that have been changed through genetic engineering.
2. The crops are healthier and grow faster. Therefore, more food can be grown in a shorter period of time. Thus, more people can be fed, and food shortages can be prevented.
3. Some people worry that we don't really know if genetically modifying food is safe for people and the environment. They are afraid that eating GM food might be harmful to their health, and that growing GM food might be harmful to the earth.

eating GM food might be harmful to their health, and that growing GM food might be harmful to the earth.

EXPANDING VOCABULARY

Studying Word Grammar, Page 118

(A)

1. I
2. T
3. I
4. T

Word Families, Page 119

Answers will vary. Possible answers include:

2. get any of their money when they die
3. help you
4. change it
5. do it again

BUILDING DICTIONARY SKILLS

Finding Collocations, Page 121

(A)

1. Follow
2. prescribed, for
3. prescription for
4. on a diet

UNIT 4: Getting Emotional

CHAPTER 10: Can You Translate an Emotion?

GETTING READY TO READ, PAGE 129

(B)

1. grief
2. guilt
3. disgust
4. cheerfulness
5. anger

READING

Comprehension Check, Page 131

Corrections for false items may vary. The number in parentheses is the paragraph number where the correct information can be found.

1. ?
2. T
3. ?
4. T
5. ?
6. F—The word *sattva* means lightness. (9)

EXPLORING VOCABULARY

Thinking about the Vocabulary, Page 132

Guessing Strategy

Reveals is similar in meaning to *not hidden*.

Unit 4, Ch. 10

Using the Vocabulary, Page 133
1. universal
2. attempted
3. particularly, observe
4. associate, reveal
5. recognize
6. In contrast, shame
7. honor
8. translate, Indeed

DEVELOPING READING SKILLS

Understanding Inference, Page 134

Answers may vary but should contain similar content.
1. They are also somewhat uncomfortable expressing these emotions, but not as uncomfortable as males in the United States.
2. They probably do not take it seriously. They might laugh at them or tell them to stop behaving so childishly. They do not react with anger.
3. They probably take it very seriously. They might be frightened and think that their child has a "demon" inside, and perhaps they will ask someone for help in getting rid of the demon. They probably are very careful to teach their children to hide their anger from others.

Paraphrasing, Page 134
1. a
2. b
3. a

EXPANDING VOCABULARY

Using the Vocabulary in New Contexts, Page 135
1. honor
2. particularly
3. associate
4. recognize
5. attempt
6. translate
7. universal
8. observe
9. indeed
10. reveal
11. shame
12. in contrast

Word Families, Page 136
1. disgusting
2. guilty
3. shameful
4. cheerful/cheery
5. angry
6. disgusted
7. ashamed

Studying Word Grammar, Page 137

(A)

Correct: 1, 4, 5, 6
Incorrect: 2, 3

CHAPTER 11: Japanese Trying Service with a Smile

GETTING READY TO READ, PAGE 140

(B)
1. e
2. a
3. b
4. d
5. c

READING

Comprehension Check, Page 142

Corrections for false items may vary. The number in parentheses is the paragraph number where the correct information can be found.
1. T
2. F—The Japanese do appreciate humor. (6)
3. T
4. F—The purpose of smile schools is to improve business during the recession. (3)
5. T
6. T

EXPLORING VOCABULARY

Thinking about the Vocabulary, Page 143

Guessing Strategy

Answers may vary but should contain similar content.
1. frown
2. to make an angry or unhappy expression
3. not considered acceptable

Using the Vocabulary, Page 144
1. proper
2. virtue
3. eyebrows
4. frowned upon
5. consciousness
6. harmony
7. humor
8. choosy
9. institute
10. artificial
11. make up for

DEVELOPING READING SKILLS

Scanning, Page 145
2. Relax your tongue.
3. Put your hands on your stomach and laugh out loud.
4. Even if you are feeling depressed, give the customers an artificial smile.
5. Bite on a chopstick.
6. Put your face under water and then breathe out while laughing.

Understanding Reference Words, Page 145
1. c
2. c
3. c, c/a
4. c, a

EXPANDING VOCABULARY

Using the Vocabulary in New Contexts, Page 146

1. make up for
2. proper
3. eyebrows
4. frowned upon
5. harmony
6. consciousness
7. artificial
8. choosy
9. institutes
10. humor
11. virtue

Word Families, Page 147

1. picky
2. juicy
3. watery
4. airy
5. smelly

Studying Phrasal Verbs, Page 147

1. b
2. d
3. c
4. a

CHAPTER 12: Road Rage

GETTING READY TO READ, PAGE 150

1. pregnant
2. slammed
3. witness
4. gesture
5. pull in front of

READING

Comprehension Check, Page 154

Corrections for false items may vary. The number in parentheses is the paragraph number where the correct information can be found.

1. F—Road rage is not a crime. (5)
2. F—Some aggressive drivers have been involved in accidents. (6–7)
3. T
4. T
5. F—Studies show that aggressive driving is very common. (7)
6. F—"The Flash" is still being tested. (8)

EXPLORING VOCABULARY

Thinking about the Vocabulary, Page 154

Guessing Strategy

Answers may vary but should contain content similar to the following:

Flash means *to suddenly shine brightly for a short time.*

Using the Vocabulary, Page 155

1. b
2. b
3. c
4. a
5. a
6. a
7. b, c
8. b
9. c
10. c
11. a
12. c

DEVELOPING READING SKILLS

Understanding Inference, Page 157

Answers will vary. Possible answers include:

1. They probably didn't know each other. Alfieri didn't stop and help Andrews. She probably wouldn't have behaved that way if she knew her.
2. No, she didn't. We know this because the text says that a witness followed her all the way to work to get her license plate number. If she had stopped, that would not have been necessary.
3. The advertisements will teach the public exactly what the number of the flashes means. Probably they will also educate the public about the dangers of road rage and explain why "the Flash" will help.

Paraphrasing, Page 157

Ⓐ

1. a
2. a
3. b

Ⓑ

Answers may vary but should include similar content.

1. It is not easy to know if more people today are driving more aggressively than they did in the past.
2. However, according to the U.S. Department of Transportation, aggressive driving is involved in 70 percent or more of the traffic deaths in the United States.

EXPANDING VOCABULARY

Using the Vocabulary in New Contexts, Page 158

1. legal
2. tragedy
3. rage
4. insurance
5. calculate
6. incident
7. accuse
8. injured
9. vehicle
10. range
11. damaged
12. flashed
13. sensational

Word Families, Page 159

Answers may vary but should include similar content.
1. showing emotions such as love, pity, and sadness too strongly
2. a feeling that you get from your senses or an experience
3. a piece of equipment that finds heat, light, or sound, even in very small amounts

Studying Collocations, Page 160
1. pick you up
2. pulled off
3. one-way street
4. take a left
5. cut him off

UNIT 4 Wrap-Up

REVIEWING READING SKILLS AND VOCABULARY

Comprehension Check, Page 163

Corrections for false items may vary. The number in parentheses is the paragraph number where the correct information can be found.
1. T
2. T
3. T
4. ?
5. F—The writer does not give an opinion. (3)

Guessing Meaning from Context, Page 164

Answers may vary but should contain similar content.
1. a condition in which your face turns very red even at just a little stress
2. something that you put on the skin of your face to look more attractive or to hide a skin condition
3. not very serious
4. tragedy; very sad

Understanding Inference, Page 164

Answers will vary. Possible answers include:
1. an actor, a doctor, a teacher
   If an actor blushes and it doesn't make sense for the character he is playing to blush, he will be at a disadvantage.
   Doctors who blush might make their patients feel uncomfortable.
   Teachers who blush all the time might make their students feel uncomfortable.
2. A woman tells the doctor that she wants the operation because she thinks she looks ugly when she blushes. The doctor asks her how often she blushes, and she says perhaps once a week—only when she feels very embarrassed.

The doctor thinks surgery isn't needed because the problem isn't serious enough.

Paraphrasing, Page 164

Answers will vary. Possible answers include:
1. If you have an expressive face, you think it is normal for people to know what you are thinking and feeling, even when you haven't spoken.
2. Many people blush when they feel embarrassed.
3. It is a serious operation. Therefore, doctors will only agree to do the surgery if the patient has tried to find other solutions to the problem.

EXPANDING VOCABULARY

Word Families, Page 165
1. gesture (V, N)
2. damage (V, N)
3. honor (V, N)
4. range (N,V)

BUILDING DICTIONARY SKILLS

Finding Words in the Dictionary, Page 166
2. injury
3. muscular
4. tragic
5. translation
6. observations
7. recognition
8. illegal
9. accusation
10. Association

UNIT 5: Man and Beast

CHAPTER 13: Is Music Universal?

GETTING READY TO READ, PAGE 169

Ⓑ
1. c
2. e
3. a
4. f
5. d
6. b

READING

Comprehension Check, Page 172

Corrections for false items may vary. The number in parentheses is the paragraph number where the correct information can be found.
1. F—No one can give an exact definition for music. (1)
2. T
3. T
4. F—Whale "songs" are remarkably similar to human songs. (4)
5. T
6. F—Almost every part of the brain is used for music. (7)

Exploring Vocabulary

Thinking about the Vocabulary, Page 173

Guessing Strategy

Answers may vary but should contain content similar to the following:

Drum means *a musical instrument with a circular frame that you play by hitting it with your hand or a stick.*

Using the Vocabulary, Page 174

1. b	8. a
2. b	9. b
3. c	10. b
4. a	11. a
5. a	12. a
6. b	13. a
7. c	

Developing Reading Skills

Understanding Main Ideas, Major Points, and Supporting Details, Page 176

Answers may vary but should contain similar content.

I. Similarities between human and animal music reveal a deep bond between living things
   A. <u>Structure of whale music and human music is very similar.</u>
      1. similar tonal scale
      2. songs have introduction and variation of theme
   B. Many bird species use music like humans
      1. songs passed from generation to generation
      2. share songs with peers
      3. use note scales similar to humans
      4. some make instruments and play them

Summarizing, Page 176

Summaries may vary but should contain similar content.

There are remarkable similarities between human and animal music. These similarities provide evidence that there is a deep bond between humans and animals. For example, whale songs and human songs share many of the same structures. Both whales and humans use similar tonal scales, and the songs of both species contain introductions and variations on a theme. Many bird species also use music in ways that are very similar to the human use of music. Like humans, some birds pass songs from one generation to the next and share songs with their peers. They also use the same tonal scales as humans. And at least one species of bird makes and plays its own musical instruments.

Expanding Vocabulary

Using the Vocabulary in New Contexts, Page 177

1. auditory	8. make sense of
2. bond	9. evidence
3. visual	10. key
4. scale	11. system
5. endless	12. structure
6. hollow	13. themes
7. drums	14. precise

Word Families, Page 178

Ⓐ

1. b	4. d
2. a	5. c
3. e	

p.179?

CHAPTER 14: Our Dogs Are Watching Us

Getting Ready to Read, Page 181

Ⓑ

1. d	4. b
2. e	5. a
3. c	

Reading

Comprehension Check, Page 184

Corrections for false items may vary. The number in parentheses is the paragraph number where the correct information can be found.

1. F—The experiments proved that dogs are better at understanding human communication than chimpanzees. (1–3)
2. T
3. F—The experiments showed that wolves and dogs are related but are different in certain ways. (4)
4. ?
5. F—The behavior of young wolves and young dogs is different. (8)
6. T

Exploring Vocabulary

Thinking about the Vocabulary, Page 185

Guessing Strategy

Striking is similar in meaning to *noticed*.

Using the Vocabulary, Page 186
1. chimpanzees
2. overall
3. evolution
4. innate, immature
5. familiarize
6. socialized
7. eliminate
8. used to
9. lid
10. fastening
11. checked out

DEVELOPING READING SKILLS

Understanding Details, Page 187
a. 1
b. 1
c. 1, 2
d. 1
e. 2
f. 1

Recognizing Tone, Page 187

Answers will vary. Possible answers include:

The writer's tone is playful, not serious. He is not really conducting research. Perhaps he uses this tone because he is writing for the general public, rather than for scientists. He is trying to make the text understandable and enjoyable for all readers. He wants to end the text with a funny image. The writer also uses a playful tone in paragraph 7.

EXPANDING VOCABULARY

Using the Vocabulary in New Contexts, Page 188
1. fasten
2. chimpanzees
3. innate
4. lid
5. domestication
6. socialization
7. eliminate → reduce
8. familiarize
9. immature
10. overall
11. check out
12. used to

Word Families, Page 189
1. a. domestic
   b. domesticate
2. a. immaturity
   b. immature
3. a. familiarity
   b. familiar
4. a. socialize
   b. socialization
5. a. evolution
   b. evolve

Studying Word Grammar, Page 190
(A)
1. get
2. get
3. is
4. am

CHAPTER 15: The Mind of the Chimpanzee

GETTING READY TO READ, PAGE 193
(B)
1. c
2. a
3. d
4. b

READING

Comprehension Check, Page 196

Corrections for false items may vary. The number in parentheses is the paragraph number where the correct information can be found.
1. F—The Gardners got an infant chimpanzee to conduct research. (1)
2. F—Chimpanzees can learn how to use sign language. (1)
3. F—Washoe learned ASL, a language used by the deaf, but she is not deaf. (1)
4. F—Dogs and chimpanzees both have good memories. (3)
5. T
6. T

EXPLORING VOCABULARY

Thinking about the Vocabulary, Page 197

Guessing Strategy
Protesting means *speaking out against.*

Using the Vocabulary, Page 198
1. infant
2. possess
3. out of sight
4. puzzled, eventually
5. combined
6. protest
7. imply
8. controversy
9. bitter
10. pile

DEVELOPING READING SKILLS

Understanding Major Points and Supporting Details, Page 199
(A)
2. SD
3. MP
4. SD
5. MP
6. MP
7. SD
8. SD

9. SD
10. MP

(B)
MP: The lives of wild chimpanzees are very complex.
SD: All chimps learn what their position in chimp society is.

MP: Chimpanzees can learn how to communicate with humans.
SD: Chimps have been taught some of the signs of ASL.
SD: Chimpanzees recognize people that they haven't seen in years.

MP: Chimps are artistically creative.
SD: Laboratory chimps like to draw and paint, and they give names to their "artwork."

MP: Chimps have good memories.
SD: Chimpanzees recognize people that they haven't seen in years.
SD: Chimps have been taught some of the signs of ASL.

MP: Chimps have some math skills.
SD: Chimps understand the meaning of *more* and *less*.

Understanding Main Ideas, Page 200
Answers may vary but should contain content similar to the following:

Years of research on chimpanzees in laboratories and in the wild have shown how remarkable our nearest animal relatives are—and how similar they are to us.

Summarizing, Page 200

Summaries will vary but should contain similar content.

Years of research on chimpanzees in laboratories and in the wild have shown how remarkable our nearest animal relatives are—and how similar they are to us. Chimps in the laboratory, for example, have been taught American Sign Language (ASL). They have proven that they can use and even create language to communicate complex ideas and feelings. It is also clear that chimps have good memories. They are able to recognize people that they haven't seen in years. Laboratory experiments have also proven that chimps have some mathematical ability. They understand the meaning of *more* and *less*. In addition, chimps can be artistic—laboratory chimps like to draw and paint, and they even name their "artwork."

Why do chimpanzees possess all of these abilities? Researchers believe that it is because the lives of wild chimpanzees are very complex. Chimpanzees, like humans, are social animals. Each member of a chimpanzee group must understand his/her social position within the group. Every day, chimps must make complex decisions, including when to hide their intentions from other chimps. To survive in this group environment, chimps must be intelligent and creative.

Using the Vocabulary in New Contexts, Page 200

1. infant
2. possess
3. out of sight
4. pile
5. protest
6. controversy
7. bitter
8. combine
9. puzzles
10. implying
11. eventually

Word Families, Page 201

2. an analytical
3. controversial
4. the implication
5. all of his possessions
6. are possessive
7. puzzled by, puzzle
8. protect wild

UNIT 5 Wrap-Up

REVIEWING READING SKILLS AND VOCABULARY

Comprehension Check, Page 204

Corrections for false items may vary. The number in parentheses is the paragraph number where the correct information can be found.

1. ?
2. T
3. F—Little Joe's behavior is normal for an 11-year-old gorilla. (4)
4. F—Little Joe was sitting at the bus stop. (1)
5. T

Guessing Meaning from Context, Page 205

1. f
2. c
3. b
4. g
5. i
6. h
7. a
8. j

Paraphrasing, Page 205

Answers will vary. Possible answers include:
1. Witness Rhonda Devance saw the gorilla too. However, she didn't realize that it was a gorilla.
2. Zoo officials did not understand how Little Joe escaped. They thought it was impossible for him to get out of the place where he was kept.
3. But they understood why he tried to escape.

EXPANDING VOCABULARY

Studying Collocations, Page 206

1. bitter wind
2. bitter argument
3. bitter disappointment
4. bitter protest
5. bitter end

PLAYING WITH WORDS, PAGE 207

Across
2. species
4. hollow
5. evolve
6. fasten

7. chimp
8. lid
9. infant
10. puzzled

Down
1. biologist
2. scale
3. journal

5. evidence
10. pile

BUILDING DICTIONARY SKILLS

Finding the Correct Meaning, Page 208
1. a. 1
   b. 2
2. a. 3
   b. 4   *c. 5*
3. a. 1 (entry 1)
   b. 2 (entry 1)
   c. 7
4. a. 3
   b. 7   *c. 2*

UNIT 6: The People Behind the Science

CHAPTER 16: A Woman's Fate

GETTING READY TO READ, PAGE 211

Ⓑ
1. gloves
2. determined
3. prestigious

4. unique
5. see the big picture

READING

Comprehension Check, Page 215
Corrections for false items may vary. The number in parentheses is the paragraph number where the correct information can be found.
1. F—Her mother worked, but she did live with her family. (2)
2. ?
3. T
4. F—Choi decided to study clothing physiology. (6)
5. ?
6. ?

EXPLORING VOCABULARY

Thinking about the Vocabulary, Page 215
Guessing Strategy
1. **Former** means *previous.*
2. **Resist** means *not agree to something.*

Using the Vocabulary, Page 216
1. fate
2. resisted
3. former
4. confirm
5. coming up with, suitable
6. well-being
7. agricultural
8. stains
9. slip
10. function
11. sweating
12. interfere

DEVELOPING READING SKILLS

Understanding Text Organization, Page 217
a. 8
b. 1
c. 2
d. 3
e. 6

f. 5
g. 4
h. 7
i. 9
j. ?

Recognizing Point of View, Page 218
1. The writer admires Jeong-wha Choi.

Summarizing, Page 218
Summaries will vary but should contain similar content.

Dr. Jeong-wha Choi is a remarkable woman. She is a scientist, inventor, wife, and mother. Choi's childhood dream was to be a wife and mother. She attended university, but she never intended to work after marriage. Fate, however, had other plans.

Choi graduated with a degree in Home Economics from Seoul National University. While she waited to find a suitable husband, she worked as a child welfare worker. Then her former professors offered her a job as their assistant. While she was working at the university, she became interested in a new academic field called clothing physiology. The field did not exist in Korea at that time, so Choi decided to study in Japan. She taught herself Japanese, and then she completed both a master's degree and a Ph.D in clothing physiology. She returned to Korea and became a professor in the Home Economics department of her former university.

Now, Choi conducts research on clothing function. She and her team have invented a variety of unique types of clothing for agricultural workers. Eventually, Choi did marry and have two children.

EXPANDING VOCABULARY

Using the Vocabulary in New Contexts, Page 218
1. stain
2. suitable
3. slip
4. interfere
5. resist
6. former
7. fate
8. well-being
9. confirm
10. agricultural
11. came up with
12. function
13. sweat

Word Families, Page 219
1. interstate
2. interlocking
3. interpersonal
4. interaction
5. interrelated

Studying Phrasal Verbs, Page 220
Answers will vary. Possible answers include:
a. come up against = to have to deal with difficult problems or people
b. come between = to cause trouble between two or more people
c. come down with = to become infected with a particular illness
d. come across = to meet someone or to discover something, usually by chance
e. come down on = to punish someone severely

CHAPTER 17: The Father of Vaccination

GETTING READY TO READ, PAGE 222

Ⓑ
1. S
2. S
3. D
4. S
5. D

READING

Comprehension Check, Page 225
Corrections for false items may vary. The number in parentheses is the paragraph number where the correct information can be found.
1. T
2. ?
3. F—He did variolate his patients, but in a more humane way. (4)
4. F—He discovered a way to prevent smallpox. (7)
5. T
6. F—Vaccination can be used to prevent many diseases, not just smallpox. (7–8)

EXPLORING VOCABULARY

Thinking about the Vocabulary, Page 226

Guessing Strategy
Turn down means *not accept.*

Using the Vocabulary, Page 227
1. practice (or procedure)
2. abuse
3. means
4. procedure (or practice)
5. contagious
6. infected
7. request, permission
8. vaccination
9. turned down
10. reviewing
11. free of

DEVELOPING READING SKILLS

Understanding Reference Words, Page 228
1. in a barn
2. the scientific method, Hunter
3. the procedure (variolation)
4. the fact that Phipps never developed smallpox
5. vaccination

Understanding Main Points and Important Details, Page 229

Answers may vary but should contain similar content.

When? When Jenner was 8 years old / *What?* Variolated against smallpox by being locked in a barn with other variolated children / *Where?* A barn in a small town in England / *Who?* Jenner, Jenner's parents, other children in Jenner's hometown

When? 1770–1772 / *What?* Studied anatomy and surgery / *Where?* St. George's Hospital in London / *Who?* Jenner, anatomy and surgery instructor John Hunter

When? 1772–May 1796 / *What?* Worked as a doctor and came up with a theory about smallpox / *Where?* Jenner's hometown / *Who?* Jenner, Jenner's patients

When? May–July 1796 / *What?* Conducted a risky experiment to test vaccination theory / *Where?* Jenner's hometown / *Who?* Jenner, Sarah Nelmes, James Phipps, James' parents, other doctors

When? End of 1796 / *What?* Wrote a report on experiments, but it wasn't published—it was turned down / *Where? . . . ?* / *Who?* The Royal Society

When? 1797–1798 / *What?* Continued experiments on vaccination / *Where? . . . ?* / *Who?* Jenner

When? 1798 / *What?* Published book on vaccination / *Where? . . . ?* / *Who?* Jenner, 23 vaccinated patients

When? 1798–beginning of the nineteenth century / *What?* Practice of vaccination spread / *Where?* London and worldwide / *Who?* Jenner, well-known London physicians, other physicians around the world

When? 1977 / *What?* Last known victim of smallpox recovered / *Where? . . . ?* / *Who?* Last known victim of smallpox

When? 1980 / *What?* Announced that the disease of smallpox had been eliminated / *Where? . . . ?* / *Who?* World Health Assembly

Summarizing, Page 230

Summaries may vary but should contain similar content.

When Edward Jenner was eight years old, he was locked in a barn with other children who were intentionally infected with the contagious disease called smallpox. This procedure was called variolation. It was done to prevent severe cases of smallpox, but it was very risky. Many children died. Fortunately, Jenner survived.

From 1770–1772, Jenner studied anatomy and surgery under John Hunter at St. George's Hospital in London. He then returned to his hometown and worked as a physician from 1772–1796. During that time, he came up with a theory about how to prevent smallpox. In 1796, he tested his theory on a young boy named James Phipps. It was a risky experiment, but it worked. Phipps never developed smallpox, even though Jenner attempted to infect him several times. At the end of 1796, Jenner wrote a paper on the procedure, which he called vaccination, and sent it to the Royal Society of London for review. They turned it down.

Jenner continued his experiments, and in 1798 he published his own book on vaccination. It was based on the cases of 23 patients that he had vaccinated. Important physicians in London read about Jenner's procedure and started using it too. By the end of the century, physicians all over the world were vaccinating their patients against smallpox.

In 1977, the last known victim of smallpox recovered, and in 1980 the World Health Assembly announced that the world was free of smallpox.

EXPANDING VOCABULARY

Using the Vocabulary in New Contexts, Page 230

1. request	7. free of
2. contagious	8. infected
3. reviewed	9. procedure
4. permission	10. vaccinations
5. means	11. abuse
6. turned down	12. practice

Word Families, Page 231
1. move or go between (Dictionary definition: to talk to someone in authority or do something in order to prevent something from happening)
2. move or go back (Dictionary definition: if something you see, hear, or feel recedes, it gets farther and farther away until it disappears)
3. go before (Dictionary definition: to happen or exist before something else)

Studying Collocations, Page 231
Answers will vary. Possible answers include:
a. a very bad or serious storm
b. very gentle and easygoing
c. not strong tasting or hot tasting
d. a not very bad or serious cold
e. very strong and serious criticism
f. very bad pain
g. not very bad pain

CHAPTER 18: A Nose for Science

GETTING READY TO READ, PAGE 234

1. fragrance, perfume, scent
2. tale, legend
3. royal
4. royalty

READING

Comprehension Check, Page 238

Corrections for false items may vary. The number in parentheses is the paragraph number where the correct information can be found.

1. ?
2. F—Turin wrote a perfume guide for consumers. (5–6)
3. T
4. F—Turin's theory is criticized within the scientific community. (9–10)
5. T
6. ?

EXPLORING VOCABULARY

Thinking about the Vocabulary, Page 238

Guessing Strategy

Answers may vary but should contain content similar to the following:

Obsessed means *thinking about someone or something all the time, so that you cannot think of anything else.*

Using the Vocabulary, Page 239

1. entertaining
2. obsessed
3. discount
4. poetic
5. secretive
6. access
7. physics
8. path
9. fraud
10. investment
11. focused
12. standards

DEVELOPING READING SKILLS

Understanding Purpose, Page 240

1. b
2. a
3. a
4. a

Summarizing, Page 241

e, f, g, h, i, j

Summaries will vary but should contain similar content.

Luca Turin is a scientist with an obsession with smell. He can smell something and almost immediately analyze its chemical composition. Collecting perfume is his hobby. His hobby, his nose, and his scientific background led him to come up with a theory of smell.

Turin believes that smell is based on the vibrations of molecules. His theory challenges the shape theory of smell (smell is based on the shapes of molecules), which many scientists believe in.

When Turin sent a paper explaining his theory to the journal *Nature*, the reviewers turned it down. They said that the theory did not make sense. Turin, however, argues that the reviewers did not understand his theory. According to him, since he used complex ideas from chemistry, physics, and biology, and since most scientists only focus on one area of science, none of the reviewers were qualified to review his data. He later published his paper in a less prestigious journal.

Turin has since started his own company. Using his theory of smell, he makes smell molecules that he sells to perfume companies. He has not yet received scientific recognition for his theory.

EXPANDING VOCABULARY

Using the Vocabulary in New Contexts, Page 241

1. obsessed
2. discount
3. standards
4. entertain
5. fraud
6. investment
7. physics
8. Access
9. path
10. focus
11. secretive
12. poetic

Word Families, Page 242

1. secretive
2. legendary
3. obsessive
4. fraudulent

PUTTING IT ALL TOGETHER

Discussion, Page 244

1. Marie Curie: e; Charles Darwin: c; Albert Einstein: a; Galileo Galilei: f; Isaac Newton: b; Louis Pasteur: d

UNIT 6 Wrap-Up

REVIEWING READING SKILLS AND VOCABULARY

Comprehension Check, Page 246

Corrections for false items may vary. The number in parentheses is the paragraph number where the correct information can be found.

1. F—Scientists are worried that not enough students are choosing careers in science and technology. (1)
2. T
3. F—Science teachers do not use enough visual images. (2)

4. F—Students don't have a chance to understand theories and relate them to their individual experiences. (3)
5. ?

Guessing Meaning from Context, Page 247
1. visual images
2. verbally
3. formula
4. To that end

Understanding Inference, Page 247
Answers may vary but should contain similar content.
1. It is possible that the writer is implying this. However, a better inference is that teachers of other subjects use more visual images than science teachers and therefore attract more students to their classes.
2. Examples of visual images include drawings, photographs, diagrams, charts, and graphs.

Summarizing, Page 247
Summaries may vary but should contain similar content.

Scientists are concerned that not enough students are choosing scientific careers. They believe that at least part of the problem comes from the way that science is taught. Although most people are visual learners, science teachers use very few visual images. Instead, they present information verbally. This makes it difficult or even impossible for many students to understand the material.

Experts in science education think that science teachers should use more visual images in their teaching. In that way, their lessons will be effective for both visual and verbal learners.

EXPANDING VOCABULARY

Studying Phrasal Verbs, Page 248
Answers may vary but should contain similar content.

1. to refuse to let people into a theater, restaurant, etc. because it is too full
2. to arrive
3. to give something you find to someone in authority so that it can be returned to the owner
4. to become something different
5. to make someone decide that she/he does not like someone or something

Word Families, Page 249
Answers may vary but should contain similar content.
1. relating to the body
2. one
3. farm or farming

BUILDING DICTIONARY SKILLS, PAGE 250

1. Circle the following: taking pictures; paints a clear picture of; be in/out of the picture; get the picture
2. Circle the following: by all means; by no means; a means to an end; a man of means
3. Circle the following: feel free; set free; free of; free from

1. feel free
2. out of the picture
3. a means to an end

UNIT TESTS

UNIT 1 TEST

Reading

Read the text and complete the exercises.

Remarkable Art?

1   MOBA is a small art museum located in the United States in a small city a few miles west of Boston. As in most art museums, the paintings at MOBA are chosen carefully. When deciding what to include in the museum, MOBA's curator looks for paintings that express something original and that are challenging or fascinating to look at. If you visit the museum, you will probably agree that each work is remarkable—that is, remarkably *bad*. MOBA, or the Museum of Bad Art, is reportedly the only museum in the world that contains just bad art.

2   Take, for example, the painting that started it all: *Lucy in the Field with Flowers*. It shows an older woman with blue hair and a serious expression on her face. She is sitting in the middle of a field of flowers on a chair with no legs. Her blue hair is blowing in the wind, but oddly, the flowers and grass are not moving. The sky is a brilliant yellow, perhaps to make her blue hair and dress stand out. *Lucy*, like many of the paintings in MOBA, was found in a trash can. But not all works in the museum are found in the trash. A surprising number of artists send in their own work. And getting a painting into the museum is competitive—the curator does not accept most of the paintings that are sent to the museum. The reason? They might be bad, but they don't stand out. In other words, they aren't bad *enough*.

3   Does it take talent to get into MOBA? It depends on your definition of talent. According to the museum's director, some of the paintings were clearly done by people who have some knowledge of artistic technique. And there is one characteristic that the curator looks for in every painting—the artist must be trying hard to express something. That "something," however, will probably remain a mystery to most MOBA visitors.

Comprehension

Read these sentences. Circle T (True) or F (False). (20 points)

1. MOBA is a large and very famous museum.	**T**	**F**
2. The painting *Lucy in the Field with Flowers* was the first painting chosen for MOBA.	**T**	**F**
3. All of the paintings in the museum were found in the trash.	**T**	**F**
4. Artists don't want their paintings to be chosen for MOBA.	**T**	**F**
5. Some of the paintings in MOBA are done by artists who know how to use artistic techniques.	**T**	**F**

Reading Skills

A. Answer the questions. (15 points)

1. In paragraph 1, the word *curator* means _____

   _____.

2. In paragraph 1, the word *work* means _____

   _____.

3. In paragraph 2, the word *oddly* means _____

   _____.

B. Complete the sentences. (15 points)

1. MOBA is remarkable because _____

   _____.

2. The painting *Lucy in the Field with Flowers* is unusual because _____

   _____.

3. Some paintings are not accepted by MOBA because _____

   _____.

C. Answer the questions. (10 points)

1. What is the topic of the reading? _____

2. What is the main idea of the reading? _____

   _____.

Vocabulary

A. Choose the word or phrase that best completes the sentence. Circle a, b, or c. (32 points)

1. I like poems in which the words are written in _____.

   a. challenge   b. rhyme   c. technique

2. His _____ was surprising. No one expected him to say that.

   a. laboratory   b. chemical   c. announcement

3. She has a great _____. Everyone enjoys spending time with her.

   a. personality   b. proof   c. challenge

4. He did not complete the project alone. Several other people
   _____ to its success.

   a. performed   b. contributed   c. scratched

5. Dr. Adams is not in his office today. He's working in his _____.

   a. technology   b. beauty   c. laboratory

6. As soon as he found out about the criminals' _____ plan, he told
   the police.

   a. rapid   b. moral   c. evil

7. The recipe _____ apples, sugar, and butter.

    a. stands by   b. calls for   c. grows out of

8. I enjoy _____ . I don't like work that is too easy.

    a. challenges   b. expressions   c. beliefs

B. Write each adjective next to its definition. There is one extra adjective. (8 points)

illiterate	clever	live	threatened	heavenly

_____ = 1. not able to read or write

_____ = 2. performed for people who are watching

_____ = 3. showing ability or skill

_____ = 4. beautiful or good

Name: _____   Date: _____

UNIT 2 Test

Reading

Read the text and complete the exercises.

A Weighty Problem

1   According to a number of studies published in recent years, there are more overweight children in the United States today than at any time in the past. During the 1990s, the rate of overweight teenagers increased by almost 50 percent. And medical data show that in 2003, about 14 percent of 6- to 11-year-olds were overweight. An additional 13 percent of children were seriously overweight, or obese.

2   Public health experts are very concerned about the long-term effects of being overweight. Research clearly shows a pattern of physical problems that begin in childhood and continue into adulthood. For example, overweight children are more likely to get diabetes (a serious condition in which the body cannot control the amount of sugar in the blood) than their thinner peers. They also tend to have breathing problems such as asthma, and they are more likely to have high blood pressure and heart problems when they become adults. In addition, surveys conducted on overweight children show that they are likely to be depressed and to have low self-esteem.

3   In order to reduce the number of overweight and obese children, experts are examining the causes of the problem. At least one explanation is the rise in unhealthy eating patterns, including the rapidly growing popularity of fast food. A lack of regular physical exercise is another likely explanation. According to U.S. government officials, Americans are spending less time exercising and more time sitting in front of the television. Government data show that 43 percent of young teenagers watch more than two hours of television a day. Finally, and perhaps most importantly, overweight parents tend to have overweight children. In 2002, almost two thirds of adults in the United States were overweight. Children who are overweight and who have a parent who is also overweight have an 80 percent chance of becoming overweight or obese as adults.

Comprehension

Read these sentences. Circle T (True) or F (False). (20 points)

1.	Most children in the United States are overweight.	**T**	**F**
2.	In the United States, obesity is becoming a very serious public health problem.	**T**	**F**
3.	Experts believe that there is a connection between being overweight and watching a lot of television.	**T**	**F**
4.	More than half of adults in the United States are overweight.	**T**	**F**
5.	Overweight children do not tend to be overweight when they become adults.	**T**	**F**

Reading Skills

A. Answer the questions. (15 points)

1. In paragraph 1, the word *obese* means _____.

2. In paragraph 2, the word *long-term* means _____

   _____.

3. In paragraph 2, the word *asthma* means _____

   _____.

B. Which of these sentences are major points and which are supporting details? Write MP (Major Point) or SD (Supporting Detail). (20 points)

_____ 1. There are more overweight children in the United States today than at any time in the past.

_____ 2. During the 1990s, the rate of overweight teenagers increased by almost 50 percent.

_____ 3. Research clearly shows a pattern of physical problems in overweight children.

_____ 4. Overweight children are more likely to have high blood pressure and heart problems when they become adults.

_____ 5. In order to reduce the number of overweight and obese children, experts are examining the causes of the problem.

C. Answer the question. (5 points)

What is the main idea of the reading? _____

_____

Vocabulary

A. Complete each statement with the correct word from the box. There is one extra word. (32 points)

aggression	anxious	attitude	background	complaints
contact	tend to	freedom	in tears	

1. Why are you so _____? Are you worried about something?

2. Please write down the name of the person we should _____ in case of emergency.

3. She was accepted to several excellent universities because of her strong educational _____.

4. I don't think that animals should be kept in zoos. I think they should have their

   _____.

5. Gifted children _____ be perfectionists. They usually are very critical of their own work.

6. The food at that restaurant was terrible. They closed down because they got so many _____.

7. The little boy was _____ because his team lost the game.

8. She is always smiling. She never gets depressed. She has a very positive
_____.

B. Write each noun next to its definition. There is one extra noun. (8 points)

aggression	literature	pressure	survey	victim

_____ = 1. angry or threatening behavior

_____ = 2. books, plays, etc. that are considered very good and that people have liked for a long time

_____ = 3. a set of questions that you ask a large number of people

_____ = 4. someone who has been attacked or hurt very badly

UNIT 3 TEST

Reading

Read the text and complete the exercises.

A Grammar Gene?

1   In the early 1990s, a group of scientists reported that they might have identified the gene that controls our ability to learn and use grammar rules. Newspapers called it the "grammar gene" and students in language classes had a new excuse to use when they failed a grammar test: "My genes made me do it!"

2   The scientists involved in the research based their conclusions on a careful examination of several generations of one unusual English family. Many individuals in the family are unable to speak and write grammatically. They also suffer from other speech and language problems, including poor pronunciation and difficulty understanding speech. The scientists became convinced that a genetic problem prevented the family from using grammar correctly. They tried to determine which gene or genes were in charge of one of the most important traits that distinguishes humans from other animals: language use.

3   In 2001, researchers finally identified the gene that is at least partly responsible for the family's severe language problems. However, they no longer believe that the gene is directly related to the ability to learn and use grammar. Instead, researchers now believe that the gene controls the brain's ability to put things into the correct order. Therefore, people with the genetic disorder have trouble putting sounds together to make words and words together to make sentences. They also have difficulty moving parts of their bodies in a specific order. For example, they have trouble following instructions to open their mouths or close their lips. This has led some researchers to theorize that the basic problem is actually movement in general, and not speech or language specifically.

4   Today, research is progressing on the causes of this uncommon disorder, but scientists agree that there is no "grammar gene." So, students who were waiting for a quick cure had better go back to studying.

Comprehension

Read these sentences. Circle T (True) or F (False). (20 points)

1. Scientists studied one family with a very unusual genetic condition.   **T**   **F**

2. Family members with the genetic disorder have grammar problems but are completely normal in every other way.   **T**   **F**

3. Today, most scientists do not believe that there is one gene that controls our ability to use grammar correctly.   **T**   **F**

4. Scientists believe that they have now identified the   **T**   **F**
   gene that controls the brain's ability to put sounds
   and movements into the correct order.

5. At first, scientists thought that the genetic disorder   **T**   **F**
   affected a very large number of people.

Reading Skills

A. Answer the questions. (15 points)

1. In paragraph 1, the word *excuse* means _____

   _____.

2. In paragraph 2, the word *distinguish* means _____

   _____.

3. In paragraph 3, the word *disorder* means _____

   _____.

B. Read the sentences from "A Grammar Gene?" Then, read the two sentences that follow. Circle the letter of the best inference based on the sentence from the reading. The numbers in parentheses are the paragraphs that the sentences come from. (10 points)

1. In 2001, researchers finally identified the gene that is at least partly responsible
   for the family's severe language problems. (3)

   a. In addition to the gene that the scientists have identified, it is possible that
      there are other genes that are involved in language use.

   b. Now that scientists have identified the cause of the family's language
      problems, they will be able to find a cure.

2. However, they no longer believe that the gene is directly related to the ability to
   learn and use grammar. (3)

   a. Some scientists used to believe that there was a gene specifically in charge of
      grammar.

   b. Scientists now believe that there is no connection between genetics and the
      ability to learn and use grammar.

C. Complete this summary of "A Grammar Gene?" (15 points)

1. Scientists studied the members of a family who suffer from _____

   _____.

2. The family members with the problem are unable to _____

   _____.

3. The scientists wanted to find out _____

   _____.

4. At first, the scientists thought that _____

   _____.

5. However, now they believe that _____

_____.

Vocabulary

A. Choose the word or phrase that best completes the sentence. Circle a, b, or c. (32 points)

1. She was very sick, but fortunately she is _____.

   a. prescribing   b. recovering   c. suffering

2. Parents and their children come from different _____.

   a. generations   b. operations   c. instructions

3. After 20 years, the truth about what really happened _____.

   a. brought up   b. led to   c. came out

4. After the earthquake, there was a severe _____ of food and medicine.

   a. cure   b. diet   c. shortage

5. For this job, a good _____ is important. You need to look clean, neat, and professional.

   a. appearance   b. courage   c. advantage

6. Dogs are not allowed in this apartment building. You will have to _____ your dog or find a new apartment.

   a. inherit   b. get rid of   c. replace

7. That car has many of the _____ that I want, but it is too expensive.

   a. cells   b. factors   c. features

8. The medication is effective for about half of the population. We don't know if it will be _____ for you or not.

   a. athletic   b. beneficial   c. restricted

B. Write each noun next to its definition. There is one extra noun. (8 points)

advantage	courage	gender	humanity	intellect

_____ = 1. the ability to understand things and think intelligently

_____ = 2. the fact of being male or female

_____ = 3. something that helps you to be better or more successful than others

_____ = 4. the ability to be brave and calm in a situation where most people would be afraid

UNIT 4 TEST

Reading

Read the text and complete the exercises.

The Emotional Lives of Animals

1   In Tanzania, a 50-year-old female chimpanzee[1] dies. Over the next few days, animal researchers observe her son sitting beside his mother's lifeless body. From time to time, he takes her hand and makes small crying sounds. Over the next three weeks, the researchers witness a rapid decline in his physical condition. Within a month, the young chimpanzee will also be dead. The cause of death? According to respected chimpanzee expert Jane Goodall, he died of grief.

2   When an elephant dies, other elephants make a circle around the dead animal and put leaves and dirt on the dead body. If the body is removed, they will begin to cry out loud. Baby elephants have been observed smelling the bones of their dead mothers. What are they doing? According to psychiatrist[2] Jeffrey Masson, these animals are clearly expressing their grief at the death of a loved one. Their behavior also reveals that they are at least in some way conscious of the meaning of death. In his book *When Elephants Weep:*[3] *The Emotional Lives of Animals,* Masson argues that animals, like humans, experience a wide range of complex emotions, including fear, grief, love, joy, jealousy, and shame.

3   Determining what a person is feeling is difficult enough. How can we possibly know what an animal is feeling? Just observe their behavior, say a growing number of scientists who study animal behavior. Like humans, animals reveal their emotions through their facial expressions and gestures, as well as through the sounds they make.

4   Until fairly recently, talking about animal consciousness and emotion was frowned upon by the scientific community. Researchers who did so were accused of being unscientific. However, today most scientists working in the field of animal behavior recognize that many animals do indeed experience emotions that in the past were only associated with humans. But there is still disagreement about which particular emotions animals feel and how deeply they feel them. They also disagree about what effect this knowledge should have on the way animals are treated.

[1]*a chimpanzee* = a very intelligent small African ape
[2]*a psychiatrist* = a doctor who studies and treats mental illness
[3]*weep* = cry

Comprehension

Read these sentences. Circle T (True) or F (False). (20 points)

1. Only human beings feel grief.   **T**   **F**
2. Jeffrey Masson's book is about the behavior of many different types of animals.   **T**   **F**
3. Animals and humans experience many of the same emotions.   **T**   **F**

4. Animals experience emotions, but they
   do not show what they are feeling.   T   F

5. Today, most experts who study animal   T   F
   behavior are convinced that animals experience emotions.

Reading Skills

A. Answer the questions. (15 points)

1. In paragraph 1, the word *lifeless* means _____

   _____.

2. In paragraph 1, the expression *from time to time* means _____

   _____.

3. In paragraph 1, the word *decline* means _____

   _____.

B. Answer the questions in your own words. There might be more than one way to answer. (10 points)

If scientists can prove that animals feel many of the same emotions as people, how might that affect the use of animals in medical testing? How might it affect zoos?

_____

_____

_____

_____

C. Read the sentences from "The Emotional Lives of Animals." Then, read the two sentences that follow. Circle the letter of the best paraphrase of the sentence from the reading. (15 points)

1. Their behavior also reveals that they are at least in some way conscious of the meaning of death.

   a. Through their behavior, animals show that they have some understanding of what death means.

   b. When an animal is unconscious, other animals often believe that it is dead.

2. Determining what a person is feeling is difficult enough.

   a. Human beings are difficult to understand.

   b. It is not easy to know what another human being is feeling.

3. Until fairly recently, talking about animal consciousness and emotion was frowned upon by the scientific community.

   a. In the past, many scientists did not want to discuss the possibility that animals experience emotions and are conscious of what they feel.

   b. Recently, scientists have become convinced that animals experience emotions and are conscious of what they feel.

Vocabulary

A. Complete each statement with the correct word from the box. There is one extra word. (32 points)

greet	in contrast	indeed	insurance	muscles
pregnant	tragedy	vehicles	virtues	

1. My furniture was badly damaged in the fire. Fortunately, my home _____ paid for the cost of replacing everything that was damaged.

2. Cars, trucks, and motorcycles are all motor _____.

3. I lifted a lot of heavy boxes yesterday. My arm _____ really hurt.

4. In some cultures, people _____ each other with a kiss. In other cultures, they shake hands.

5. Two children died in the accident. It was a terrible _____.

6. Mike is a wonderful person. He has many _____, including honesty and kindness.

7. She is _____. The baby will be born in September.

8. Japan is an island nation, surrounded by ocean on all sides. Switzerland, _____, is surrounded by land.

B. Write each adjective next to its definition. There is one extra adjective. (8 points)

artificial	choosy	legal	proper	reserved

_____ = 1. allowed, ordered, or approved by law

_____ = 2. unwilling to express your emotions or talk about your problems

_____ = 3. not natural or sincere

_____ = 4. difficult to please

Name: _____ Date: _____

UNIT 5 TEST

Reading

Read the text and complete the exercises.

Guide Dogs for the Blind

1　　A guide dog is a dog that is trained to assist the blind. We have evidence of dogs' helping the blind going as far back as the Middle Ages.[1] But the idea of formally training dogs for this purpose is a relatively new one.

2　　One of the first guide dog training schools began in Potsdam, Germany, in 1916. At first, the dogs were trained to help the thousands of World War I soldiers blinded by poison gas. Soon, people outside of Germany heard about the school, including an American dog trainer named Dorothy Eustis. Mrs. Eustis visited the school and familiarized herself with the techniques for training guide dogs. She also wrote an article about the school for a popular American magazine, *The Saturday Evening Post.* A young blind man named Morris Frank read the article. He contacted Mrs. Eustis and convinced her to train one of her dogs for him. Eventually, Mr. Frank would open the first guide dog training school in the United States, the Seeing Eye.

3　　Training a dog to work with the blind calls for great patience and skill. Not every dog possesses the qualities necessary to become a guide dog. Key traits include intelligence, a calm personality, and the ability to form a close bond with people. Guide dogs must be able to make sense of unfamiliar places and situations. They must be able to follow precise commands[2] quickly, but they must also be intelligent enough to know when to disobey a command that might put their owner in danger.

4　　The training process has several stages. The dogs must be fully socialized before they can live with a blind person, so the first step is for immature dogs to live with a family until they are about a year old. Then, the dogs are sent to a training school. Many dogs are eliminated from the training program when it becomes obvious that they lack the innate characteristics that a guide dog must have. Dogs that successfully complete the training period are placed with[3] a blind person. Usually, the two develop a deep, lifelong bond. In fact, many blind people consider their relationship with their dogs one of the most meaningful relationships in their lives.

[1] the *Middle Ages* = the period in European history between the fifth and fifteenth centuries A.D.

[2] a *command* = an order that must be obeyed

[3] *place with* = put someone or something in a particular situation

Comprehension

Read these sentences. Circle T (True) or F (False). (20 points)

1. People started using dogs to help the blind in the twentieth century.　　　　**T**　　　　**F**

2. The first guide dog training school was started by an American.　　　　**T**　　　　**F**

3. With the proper training, almost any dog can become   **T**   **F**
   a good guide dog.

4. The training of a guide dog is complex and takes a   **T**   **F**
   long time.

5. It is important for guide dogs and their owners to form   **T**   **F**
   a close bond.

Reading Skills

A. Answer the questions. (15 points)

1. In paragraph 1, the word *assist* means_____

   _____ .

2. In paragraph 2, the word *article* means _____

   _____ .

3. In paragraph 3, the word *disobey* means _____

   _____ .

B. Fill in the missing information in the outline. The Roman numerals I, II, and III are for the major points, and the letters A, B, C, D, E, and F are for the supporting details. (25 points)

   I. <u>The first guide dog training schools</u>_____

      A. <u>Potsdam, Germany—for soldiers blinded in World War I</u>_____

      B. _____

  II. _____

      A. <u>intelligence</u>_____

      B. _____

      C. _____

      D. <u>able to make sense of unfamiliar places and situations</u>_____

      E. _____

      F. _____

 III. _____

      A. _____

      B. _____

      C. _____

      D. <u>placed with a blind person</u>_____

Vocabulary

A. Complete each statement with the correct word from the box. There is one extra word. (32 points)

back up	endless	eventually	infant	lid
overall	pile	puzzled	striking	

1. Her parents died when she was an _____, so her grandparents raised her.

2. Your son did poorly on his last test, but _____ he is doing well in the class.

3. You need to close the _____ of the paint can tightly. If you don't, the paint will dry up.

4. When you write an essay, you need to _____ your main points with details that support them.

5. Please be more careful about how much you spend. Your father and I do not have an _____ amount of money!

6. I am _____ by your change of attitude. At first you were happy about the trip, but now you say that you don't want to go. I don't understand you at all.

7. Her dark hair and eyes are _____. When she walks into a room, everyone notices her.

8. I need to organize the _____ of papers on my desk. It is such a mess that I can't find anything.

B. Write each verb next to its definition. There is one extra verb. (8 points)

fasten	imply	possess	protest	stretch

_____ = 1. to say or do something publicly to show that you disagree with something or think it is unfair

_____ = 2. to suggest that something is true without saying or showing it directly

_____ = 3. to own or have something

_____ = 4. to join together the two sides of something so that it is closed

UNIT 6 TEST

Reading

Read the text and complete the exercises.

Child Inventors

1   At an age when most children are climbing trees, Raymond Kurzweil was designing a computer program that could perform complex calculations. It functioned so well that IBM, the famous computer company, bought it from him. He was just 12 years old, but even more surprising, he designed his program in the early 1960s, at a time when most adults didn't even know what a computer looked like. He has since patented[1] a number of inventions, including the Kurzweil Reading Machine, the first machine that could actually read printed documents out loud. Many years later, Kurzweil is still coming up with brilliant inventions, and in 2002 he was admitted to the National Inventors Hall of Fame.[2]

2   Although Kurzweil's success makes him somewhat unusual, child inventors are more common than you might imagine. Take, for example, fifth-grader Wendy Johnecheck. When her teacher instructed her class to write about a famous inventor, Wendy asked for permission to come up with her own invention instead. Her teacher agreed to her request, and Wendy went to work. Her invention, the Quadro Jump, is designed to improve the popular game of jumping rope.[3] Normally, for one child to jump rope, two children are needed to turn the rope—one at each end of the rope. With the Quadro Jump, four ropes are fastened at one end to a pole. When the pole is put into the ground, four games of jump rope can be played with only four children holding the ropes instead of eight. As a result, more children are free to jump.

3   The idea for nine-year-old Brett Ruvolo's invention was also born on the playground. Brett noticed that many young baseball players wait a little too long to put their hand up to catch a ball. He came up with the idea of fastening a baseball cap and glove together with a string. When players wearing Brett's invention look up to catch a ball, the string pulls on their glove. This reminds them to put their glove in the air as soon as they look up.

4   Not all child inventions involve entertainment, however. Jenna Leone, nine, came up with a unique design for a car seatbelt that is suitable for hot climates. Her idea was to replace the metal part of the seatbelt with plastic, so that wearers will not burn themselves on the hot metal. And ten-year-old Nathan Weinberg invented a telephone answering machine that begins playing your phone messages as soon as you enter your front door.

(continued)

[1]*patent* = obtain a special document that says you have the right to make or sell a new invention or product and that no one else is allowed to do so

[2]*National Inventors Hall of Fame* = an organization in the United States that awards inventors who are involved in important technological progress

[3]*a rope* = a very strong, thick string, made by twisting pieces of thread (a long, thin line of cotton, silk, etc. that you use to sew cloth) together

5   These young inventors may never receive the prestigious National Medal[4] of Technology, as former child prodigy[5] Raymond Kurzweil did in 1999. However, with their accomplishments they have proven that it is never too early to start on the path to success.

[4]a *medal* = a round, flat piece of metal given as a prize to someone who has won a competition or done something brave

[5]a *child prodigy* = a young person who is extremely good at doing something

Comprehension

Read these sentences. Circle T (True) or F (False). (20 points)

1. Raymond Kurzweil was a very gifted child.   **T**   **F**

2. Wendy Johnecheck's invention helps children to jump very high.   **T**   **F**

3. Brett Ruvolo's invention helps young baseball players improve their game.   **T**   **F**

4. Jenna Leone's and Nathan Weinberg's inventions are very useful in everyday life.   **T**   **F**

5. All of the child inventors in the reading received the National Medal of Technology.   **T**   **F**

Reading Skills

A. Answer the questions. For number 1, you can draw a picture. (15 points)

1. In paragraph 2, the word *pole* means _____
   _____.

2. In paragraph 3, the word *playground* means _____
   _____.

3. In paragraph 5, the word *accomplishments* means _____
   _____.

B. Draw pictures of these inventions. (10 points)

1. The Quadro Jump | 2. Brett Ruvolo's invention

C. What do the boldfaced words refer to? Look back at the reading and write your answers. (15 points)

1. Her teacher agreed to **her request**, and Wendy went to work. (paragraph 2)

   her request = _____

2. **This** reminds them to put their glove in the air as soon as they look up. (paragraph 3)

   This = _____

3. **These young inventors** may never receive the prestigious National Medal of Technology (paragraph 5)

   These = _____

Vocabulary

A. Choose the word or phrase that best completes the sentence. Circle a, b, or c. (32 points)

1. Your father and I are concerned about your _____. We think that you are working too hard.

   a. well-being   b. access   c. fraud

2. Don't worry. You won't get sick. My illness is not _____.

   a. contagious   b. former   c. suitable

3. Oh no! There's a _____ on this shirt. I'll have to change.

   a. function   b. legend   c. stain

4. My grandfather likes to tell me the same _____ that his mother told him when he was young.

   a. standards   b. tales   c. scents

5. Look at me when I'm talking to you. Don't _____ me!

   a. ignore   b. confirm   c. review

6. I shop at large _____ stores because they have the best prices.

   a. unique   b. discount   c. secretive

7. Buying a house is a good _____. When you sell it, you usually make a lot of money.

   a. royalty   b. investment   c. fate

8. I don't know why they _____ my request. They just said "no." They didn't explain their decision.

   a. confirmed   b. turned down   c. came up with

B. Write each verb next to its definition. There is one extra verb. (8 points)

focus	interfere	resist	slip	sweat

_____ = 1. to have liquid coming out through your skin, especially when you are hot or nervous

_____ = 2. to accidentally move a short distance

_____ = 3. to deliberately get involved in a situation when you are not wanted or needed

_____ = 4. to pay special attention to a particular person or thing

UNIT TESTS ANSWER KEY

UNIT 1 TEST

Comprehension

Corrections for false items may vary. The number in parentheses is the paragraph number where the correct information can be found.

1. F—MOBA is a small museum. (1)   2. T   3. F—Some of the paintings in the museum were found in the trash. (2)   4. F—Some artists send their paintings to the museum's curator. (2)   5. T

Reading Skills

A. Answers will vary. Possible answers include:

1. the person at a museum who chooses the art that will be shown in the museum.   2. painting.   3. strangely; unusually.

B. Answers will vary. Possible answers include:

1. it is a museum that contains only bad art.   2. her hair is blowing in the wind, but the flowers and grass are not moving. Also, her hair is blue and the sky is yellow.   3. they aren't bad enough, or the curator doesn't feel that the artist was trying hard to express something.

C. Answers may vary but should contain similar content.

1. The topic is the Museum of Bad Art (MOBA).   2. MOBA is a very unusual museum.

Vocabulary

A. 1. b   2. c   3. a   4. b   5. c   6. c   7. b   8. a

B. 1. illiterate   2. live   3. clever   4. heavenly

UNIT 2 TEST

Comprehension

Corrections for false items may vary. The number in parentheses is the paragraph number where the correct information can be found.

1. F—Only about 27 percent of children in the United States were overweight in 2003. (1)   2. T   3. T   4. T   5. F—Overweight children do tend to be overweight when they become adults. (3)

Reading Skills

A. Answers may vary but should contain similar content.

1. seriously overweight.   2. continuing for a long period of time into the future.   3. a physical condition that causes difficulties in breathing.

B. 1. MP   2. SD   3. MP   4. SD   5. MP

C. Answers may vary but should contain content similar to the following:

The problem of overweight and obese children is becoming a serious public health problem in the United States.

Vocabulary

A. 1. anxious   2. contact   3. background   4. freedom   5. tend to   6. complaints   7. in tears   8. attitude

B. 1. aggression   2. literature   3. survey   4. victim

UNIT 3 TEST

Comprehension

Corrections for false items may vary. The number in parentheses is the paragraph number where the correct information can be found.

1. T   2. F—They also have problems with pronunciation, mouth movement, and understanding speech. (2–3)   3. T   4. T   5. F—It is an uncommon disorder. (4)

Reading Skills

A. Answers may vary but should contain similar content.

1. a reason that you give to explain why you did something wrong.

2. to understand the difference between two things, people, etc.

3. a condition that prevents part of your body from working correctly.

B. 1. a   2. a

C. Summaries may vary but should contain similar content.

1. a genetic disorder.   2. speak or write with correct grammar. They also have problems understanding speech.   3. which gene or genes were responsible for their problem.   4. the gene or genes causing the disorder was specifically related to their inability to learn and use grammar. 5. the disorder is not specifically related to language use. Instead, they believe that the gene involved in the family's disorder controls the brain's ability to put words, sounds, and movements into the correct order.

Vocabulary

A. 1. b   2. a   3. c   4. c   5. a   6. b   7. c   8. b

B. 1. intellect   2. gender   3. advantage   4. courage

UNIT 4 TEST

Comprehension

Corrections for false items may vary. The number in parentheses is the paragraph number where the correct information can be found.

1. F—Many animals, including chimpanzees and elephants, feel grief. (1–2)   2. T   3. T   4. F—Animals reveal their emotions through their facial expressions and gestures, as well as through the sounds they make. (3)   5. T

Reading Skills

A. 1. dead or seeming to be dead.   2. sometimes, but not regularly or very often.   3. to decrease in quality, quantity, importance, etc.

B. Answers may vary but should contain content similar to the following:

People may feel that if animals can feel pain, like people, they shouldn't be used for medical testing. They may also feel that it is cruel to put animals in zoos. In short, people may feel that we shouldn't do anything to animals that we wouldn't do to people.

C. 1. a   2. b   3. a

Vocabulary

A. 1. insurance   2. vehicles   3. muscles   4. greet   5. tragedy   6. virtues   7. pregnant
8. in contrast

B. 1. legal   2. reserved   3. artificial   4. choosy

UNIT 5 TEST

Comprehension

Corrections for false items may vary. The number in parentheses is the paragraph number where the correct information can be found.
1. F—Dogs have been used to help the blind since at least the Middle Ages. (1)   2. F—The first guide dog training school was started by Germans. (2)   3. F—Many dogs do not have the traits to be a good guide dog. (3)   4. T   5. T

Reading Skills

A. Answers may vary but should contain similar content.

1. help.   2. a piece of writing in a newspaper, magazine, etc.   3. to refuse to do what you are told to do.

B. Answers may vary but should contain similar content.

   I. <u>The first guide dog training schools</u>
      A. Potsdam, Germany—for soldiers blinded in World War I
      B. The Seeing Eye in the United States—started by a blind man, Morris Frank

  II. The qualities that a good guide dog needs
      A. <u>Intelligence</u>
      B. a calm personality
      C. the ability to form a close bond with people
      D. <u>able to make sense of unfamiliar places and situations</u>

    E. able to follow precise commands quickly

    F. know when to disobey a dangerous command

    III. The training process

        A. immature dogs live with a family until one year old

        B. go to training school

        C. successfully complete training school

        D. <u>placed with a blind person</u>

Vocabulary

A. 1. infant 2. overall 3. lid 4. back up 5. endless 6. puzzled 7. striking 8. pile

B. 1. protest 2. imply 3. possess 4. fasten

UNIT 6 TEST

Comprehension

Corrections for false items may vary. The number in parentheses is the paragraph number where the correct information can be found.

1. T 2. F—It gives more children a chance to jump. (2) 3. T 4. T 5. F—Kurzweil received it. They may never receive it. (5)

Reading Skills

A. Answers may vary but should contain similar content.

1. a long stick or post. 2. a small area of land, usually next to a school or in a park, where children can play. 3. something you are able to achieve or are able to do well, especially after a lot of effort.

B. Drawings will vary but should contain similar content.

1. The Quadro Jump: Should show a long pole with four ropes attached to it. Show at least one child holding the end of one rope and another child jumping.

2. Brett Ruvolo's invention: Should show a person wearing a baseball cap and baseball glove. A string between the cap and glove should be visible.

C. 1. Wendy asked for permission to come up with her own invention. 2. when the string pulls on their glove 3. Wendy Johnecheck, Brett Ruvolo, Jenna Leone, Nathan Weinberg

Vocabulary

A. 1. a 2. a 3. c 4. b 5. a 6. b 7. b 8. b

B. 1. sweat 2. slip 3. interfere 4. focus

QUICK ORAL REVIEW

Have students look at the list of target words and phrases on the page indicated. Ask students, "Which word or phrase means . . . "

Chapter 1: What Is Anime?, Page 6

1. relating to what is right and wrong, and to the difference between good and evil? *moral*
2. done very quickly or happening in a short time? *rapid*
3. not copied or not based on something else? *original*
4. a quality that things, places, or people have that makes them very attractive to look at? *beauty*
5. things that are new, exciting, or difficult that need a lot of skill and effort to do? *challenges*
6. the quality of being liked or supported by a large number of people? *popularity*
7. has a very good natural ability? *talented*
8. things such as computers, cell phones, and fax machines? *technology*
9. not simple? *complex*
10. taking part in an activity or event? *involved*

Chapter 2: The Scientist and the Stradivarius, Page 16

1. because of? *due to*
2. facts and information that prove something is true? *proof*
3. an explanation for something that may be reasonable, but has not yet been proven to be true? *theory*
4. the feeling that something is definitely true or definitely exists? *belief*
5. the act of telling people something publicly? *announcement*
6. very bright and strong? *brilliant*
7. showing skill or imagination in the arts? *artistic*
8. decides what to do, say, or believe and does not change this? *stands by*
9. not able to read or write? *illiterate*
10. the information and understanding that you have gained through learning and experience? *knowledge*

Chapter 3: The History of Rap, Page 27

1. tried to win or gain something or tried to be better or more successful than someone else? *competed*
2. helped make something happen? *contributed*
3. someone's character, especially the way he or she behaves toward other people? *personality*
4. talked to other people and worked together with them? *interacted*
5. showing ability or skill, especially in making things? *clever*
6. special methods of doing things? *techniques*
7. the tools, machines, or instruments that you need for a particular activity? *equipment*
8. a special quality or feature that someone or something has? *characteristic*
9. turning around and around very quickly? *spinning*
10. performed for people who are watching? *live*

Have students look at the list of target words and phrases on the page indicated. Ask students, "Which word or phrase means . . . "

Chapter 4: Sleepy Teens, Page 48

1. crying? *in tears*
2. statements in which you say you are annoyed, not satisfied, or unhappy about someone or something? *complaints*
3. probably or almost definitely? *likely*
4. stay awake? *stay up*
5. people who have responsible positions in organizations? *officials*
6. a feeling of worry about something important? *concern*
7. became smaller or less in size, amount, or price? *reduced*
8. a scientific test done to show how something or someone will react in a situation, or to prove that an idea is true? *experiment*
9. not less than a certain number or amount? *at least*
10. the state of not having something or not having enough of something? *lack*

Chapter 5: Growing Up Gifted, Page 58

1. having the natural ability to do something well? *gifted*
2. give most of your attention to one thing? *concentrate on*
3. able to understand the feelings and problems of other people? *sensitive*
4. a situation in which people are treated very unfairly? *injustice*
5. arranged for a book, magazine, or newspaper to be written, printed, and sold? *published*
6. people who are the same age as you, or who have the same type of job or rank? *peers*
7. the conditions of your work, family, or way of living that cause problems and make you worry? *pressure*
8. to be likely to do something? *tend to*
9. judging people or things, sometimes in an unfair way? *critical*
10. succeeded in doing or getting something after trying hard? *achieved*

Chapter 6: School Bullies, Page 70

1. because of a certain fact or reason? *on the basis of*
2. looked at something carefully in order to make a decision or find out something? *examined*
3. communicate with a person, organization, or country? *contact*
4. too heavy or too fat? *overweight*
5. the opinions and feelings that you usually have about a certain idea, thing, or person? *attitude*
6. supporting or defending someone or something when he or she is being attacked or criticized? *standing up for*
7. did something in order to find out or prove something? *conducted*
8. a set of questions that you ask a large number of people in order to find out about their opinions and behavior? *survey*
9. the type of education, experiences, and family that someone has? *background*
10. information or facts? *data*

UNIT 3: GENETICS: THE SCIENCE OF WHO WE ARE

Have students look at the list of target words and phrases on the page indicated. Ask students, "Which word or phrase means . . . "

Chapter 7: The Science of Genetics, Page 89

1. all the people who are about the same age, especially in a family? *generation*
2. knew or understood the importance of something that you did not know before? *realized*
3. stop something from happening or someone from doing something? *prevent*
4. start doing something or be used instead of another person or thing? *replace*
5. remove something or someone that is bad from a place, organization, or system? *get rid of*
6. make an injury or illness better, so that the person who was sick is well? *cure*
7. the smallest parts of an animal or plant that can live on their own? *cells*
8. find out the facts about something? *determine*
9. get a quality, type of behavior, or physical characteristic from one of your parents? *inherit*
10. information that tells you how to do something? *instructions*

Chapter 8: Designing the Future, Page 100

1. good enough for a certain purpose? *acceptable*
2. made something happen or exist as a result of something else? *led to*
3. able to play one sport or a lot of sports very well? *athletic*
4. the way someone or something looks or seems to other people? *appearance*
5. moving closer to someone or something? *approaching*
6. things that help you to be better or more successful than others? *advantages*
7. certain that something is true? *convinced*
8. in fact, although it may seem strange? *actually*
9. find out exactly what the cause or origin of something is? *identify*
10. starts to talk about something or someone? *brings up*

Chapter 9: A Drug to Match Your Genes, Page 111

1. developing, improving, or becoming more complete over a period of time? *progressing*
2. producing the result that was wanted? *effective*
3. good or helpful? *beneficial*
4. in control of or responsible for? *in charge of*
5. experiencing something bad, such as pain, sickness, or the effects of a bad situation? *suffering*
6. lucky? *fortunate*
7. causing hurt to someone or something? *harmful*
8. had something in your mind as a plan or purpose? *intended*
9. getting better after an illness or shock? *recovering*
10. some of several things that influence or cause a situation? *factors*

Have students look at the list of target words and phrases on the page indicated. Ask students, "Which word or phrase means . . . "

Chapter 10: Can You Translate an Emotion?, Page 132

1. tried to do something? *attempted*

2. especially? *particularly*

3. know someone or something that you have seen before? *recognize*

4. watch someone or something carefully? *observe*

5. the respect that someone receives from other people? *honor*

6. show something that was previously hidden? *reveal*

7. the feeling of being guilty or embarrassed that you have after doing something that is wrong? *shame*

8. concerning all the members of a group or of the world? *universal*

9. extreme sadness, especially because someone you love has died? *grief*

10. used when comparing objects or situations that are completely different from each other? *in contrast*

Chapter 11: Japanese Trying Service with a Smile, Page 143

1. done in a way so that people can hear your voice? *out loud*

2. a situation in which people are friendly and peaceful and agree with each other? *harmony*

3. the lines of short hairs above your eyes? *eyebrows*

4. unwilling to express your emotions or talk about your problems? *reserved*

5. an organization that has a particular purpose, such as scientific, educational, or medical work? *institute*

6. the ability to laugh at things and think that they are funny? *humor*

7. correct, or right for a particular situation? *proper*

8. disapproved of something? *frowned upon*

9. make a bad situation or event seem better? *make up for*

10. the understanding that you or a group of people have about a situation? *consciousness*

Chapter 12: Road Rage, Page 155

1. money paid to a company that then agrees to pay an amount of money if something bad happens to you or your property? *insurance*

2. allowed, ordered, or approved by law? *legal*

3. make a statement saying that someone has done something wrong or illegal? *accuse*

4. hurt? *injured*

5. something unusual, serious, or violent that happens? *incident*

6. harm someone or something, so that it is broken or injured? *damage*

7. finds out something or measures something using numbers? *calculates*

8. an event that is extremely sad, especially one that involves death? *tragedy*

9. intended to excite or shock people? *sensational*

10. a strong feeling of anger that you cannot control? *rage*

UNIT 5: MAN AND BEAST

Have students look at the list of target words and phrases on the page indicated. Ask students, "Which word or phrase means . . . "

Chapter 13: Is Music Universal?, Page 173

1. a feeling or interest that unites two or more people, groups, or animals? *bond*
2. very important or necessary for success or for understanding? *key*
3. exact and correct in every detail? *precise*
4. the way in which the parts of something connect with each other to form a whole? *structure*
5. a set of related or connected things that work together as a single unit? *system*
6. having an empty space inside? *hollow*
7. facts, objects, or signs that make you believe that something exists or is true? *evidence*
8. understands? *makes sense of*
9. a scientist who studies living things? *biologist*
10. a musical instrument that you play by hitting it with your hand or a stick? *drum*

Chapter 14: Our Dogs Are Watching Us, Page 185

1. get rid of something completely? *eliminate*
2. part of your character since you were born? *innate*
3. a cover for a pot, box, or other container? *lid*
4. unusual or interesting enough to be noticed? *striking*
5. easy to notice or understand? *obvious*
6. show that something is true? *back up*
7. generally? *overall*
8. joined the two sides of something together so that it is closed? *fastened*
9. looking at someone or something because he, she, or it is interesting or attractive? *checking out*
10. not fully formed or developed? *immature*

Chapter 15: The Mind of the Chimpanzee, Page 197

1. after a long time? *eventually*
2. own or have something? *possess*
3. serious, useful, or important? *meaningful*
4. a serious disagreement among many people over a plan or decision over a long period of time? *controversy*
5. suggested that something is true without saying or showing it directly? *implied*
6. say or do something publicly to show that you disagree with something or think that it is unfair? *protest*
7. a large group of similar things collected or put together? *pile*
8. a baby, especially one that cannot walk? *infant*
9. made someone confused and unable to understand something? *puzzled*
10. an area that is natural and not controlled or changed by people? *the wild*

UNIT 6: THE PEOPLE BEHIND THE SCIENCE

Have students look at the list of target words and phrases on the page indicated. Ask students, "Which word or phrase means . . . "

Chapter 16: A Woman's Fate, Page 216

1. a power that some people believe controls what happens in your life? *fate*

2. having a particular position before, but not now? *former*

3. marks on something that are difficult to remove? *stains*

4. a feeling of being comfortable, healthy, and happy? *well-being*

5. think of an idea, plan, or reply? *come up with*

6. said or proved that something is definitely true? *confirmed*

7. the usual purpose of something, or the job that someone usually does? *function*

8. deliberately get involved in a situation? *interfere*

9. right or acceptable for a particular purpose or situation? *suitable*

10. used in farming or about farming? *agricultural*

Chapter 17: The Father of Vaccination, Page 226

1. doctors? *physicians*

2. the act of allowing someone to do something? *permission*

3. didn't pay any attention to someone or something? *ignored*

4. intentionally; not happening by accident; planned? *deliberately*

5. the act of asking for something politely or formally? *request*

6. can be passed from person to person by touch or through the air? *contagious*

7. examined, considered, and judged a situation or process carefully? *reviewed*

8. a method, system, or object that is used for doing something? *means*

9. something that people do often and in a particular way? *practice*

10. cruel or violent treatment of someone, usually by someone in a position of authority? *abuse*

Chapter 18: A Nose for Science, Page 239

1. do something that interests and amuses people? *entertain*

2. a reduction in the usual price of something? *discount*

3. levels of quality, skill, or ability that are considered to be acceptable? *standards*

4. the ability, chance, or right to use something? *access*

5. a narrow road that people walk along over an area of ground? *path*

6. the study of physical objects and natural forces such as light, heat, and movement? *physics*

7. pleasant smells? *fragrances*

8. a liquid with a strong, pleasant smell that you put on your skin? *perfume*

9. something that you buy or do because it will be more valuable or useful later? *investment*

10. an old, well-known story, often about brave people or adventures? *legend*